P9-DTL-989

LATERAL LOGIC PUZZLES

THE THINKER

Erwin Brecher

Illustrated by Lucy Corvino

 Sterling Publishing Co., Inc.   New York

DEDICATION

To Ellen

*For providing the tranquility and
comfort needed to prime
the creative mind*

Edited by Claire Bazinet

Library of Congress Cataloging-in-Publication Data

Brecher, Erwin.
    Lateral logic puzzles / Erwin Brecher : illustrated by Lucy
Corvino.
        p.   cm.
    Includes index.
    ISBN 0-8069-0618-9
    1. Philosophical recreations.   2. Logic.   3. Puzzles.
I. Corvino, Lucy.   II. Title.
GV1507.P43B74   1994
793.73—dc20   94-18776
                                                                      CIP

10   9   8   7   6   5

Published by Sterling Publishing Company, Inc.
387 Park Avenue South, New York, N.Y. 10016
© 1994 by Erwin Brecher
Distributed in Canada by Sterling Publishing
% Canadian Manda Group, P.O. Box 920, Station U
Toronto, Ontario, Canada M8Z 5P9
Distributed in Great Britain and Europe by Cassell PLC
Villiers House, 41/47 Strand, London WC2N 5JE, England
Distributed in Australia by Capricorn Link (Australia) Pty Ltd.
P.O. Box 6651, Baulkham Hills, Business Centre, NSW 2153, Australia
Manufactured in the United States of America
All rights reserved

Sterling ISBN 0-8069-0618-9

CONTENTS

ACKNOWLEDGMENTS

Sources for this type of puzzle are relatively rare. Consequently, many Lateral Logic Puzzles had to be invented and I spent many sleepless nights racking my brains. I also became a scourge to friends and relatives cajoling them to contribute. Although the response was less than overwhelming, I am grateful for small mercies. In addition, I am indebted to the following authors and/or publishers whose material has been helpful and inspiring:

Victor Serebriakoff—A *Mensa Puzzle Book*
Martin Gardner
Scot Morris—*Omni Games*
P. Carter and K. Russell
Eugene P. Northrop
Gyles Brandreth

Les Smith assisted in producing original ideas and in being the devil's advocate in critiquing puzzles of my own construction. Jennifer Iles coped most efficiently with numerous changes and revisions.

INTRODUCTION

The problems in this book are generally in the form of a narrative, telling a story that seems out of kilter in some way. It may seem wildly improbable or contradictory; it may even describe bizarre or otherwise inexplicable conduct and occasionally appear to defy the laws of physics! But there are rational explanations for the stories, and the challenge is to find that explanation.

In addition to irrelevancies, the puzzles are constructed in a manner which will make the circumstances fit one, and only one, reasonable and logical solution. To help you towards that target answer, clues are provided at two levels.

Section A clues point you in the direction your thought processes should take to approach the solution. If this first clue leads to success, you can be considered a brilliant puzzlist. Even if you proceed to your section B clue, finding the answer is no mean feat. When at last you look at the solution, your surprise at how well it fits the circumstances of the story will be tinged with some disappointment if you did not think of it yourself. But wait, the fun is not over.

Once you have uncovered the solutions, with or without clues, Lateral Logic Puzzles has a second life, as a challenging parlor game.

This time, knowing the answers, you may assume the role of moderator and read the stories to friends or family, who are invited to arrive at the solutions by asking questions which you, as moderator, can answer with either "yes" or "no," or sometimes "irrelevant," until one of the players has discovered the solution. If more than three friends or family members want to participate, players can split into groups who are permitted to consult among themselves. (With groups especially, the competitive challenge can be enhanced by introducing point-scoring rules.)

The key to success is an intelligent and methodical approach to formulating questions, which should be designed to narrow the field in successive steps, almost like a forensic exercise.

While solving these puzzles is usually quite tough, creating new ones along similar lines need not be, once players have developed an understanding of what makes the puzzles tick. Devotees should therefore be able to keep the parlor game going after the examples I provide are exhausted. Indeed, I am looking forward to a flood of ideas from my readers, which will be gratefully acknowledged.

ERWIN BRECHER

PUZZLES

Dusk or Dawn 1

Norman Bronstein, a sports enthusiast and loner, would try anything that presented a physical challenge of endurance and danger. On this occasion, white-water rafting in the Amazon, he set off alone from Manaus one winter morning. At first all went well, but early in the afternoon his raft entered some rapids and struck a rock, and Norman was thrown clear onto the shore. His raft and all his belongings, including his pocket watch, were lost.

He lay for days, unconscious from a head wound. When he finally came to, it was twilight. Although dazed, Norman realized that it was dusk and that he would have to spend another night before he could be rescued. How did he know instantly that it was dusk and not dawn?

Spring in the Mountains   2

A hiker, during a vacation, discovered the bodies of a middle-aged couple, holding hands, in a remote field near the Austrian village of St. Anton. Suicide was ruled out, there was no visible evidence of cause of death that would indicate murder, nor was any poison found on medical examination. How did the couple die?

Winter Time   3

A rich bachelor, living in a ten-room apartment in Manhattan, had a clock in every room. One Saturday evening in October he reset all the clocks for winter time before going to bed. Next morning he discovered that only two clocks showed the correct time. Explain.

The Explorers   4

Two field workers were sent from a base to explore a mineral find in a remote area. They were about to collect samples when they were attacked by vicious animals. They immediately stopped working to return to the safety of their home base. One of the explorers withdrew extremely slowly, keeping a watchful eye on the animals. The other panicked and fled at great speed. Although the panicked explorer escaped being attacked, he died as soon as he reached the base, while his colleague survived. Explain.

Avoiding the Train   5

A man was walking along a railway track when he spotted an express train speeding towards him. To avoid it, he jumped off the track, but before he jumped he ran ten feet towards the train. Why?

The Paris Fair   6

Catherine and her brother, Paul, arrived in Paris from New York the day before the official opening of the World's Fair. They checked in at the Ritz, Paul occupying Room 13 and Catherine one floor higher at Number 25.

Though exhausted from the long trip, they decided to have a light dinner in the grill room before retiring. Halfway through the meal Paul could hardly keep his eyes open, showing extreme fatigue, so he decided to go to his room, leaving Catherine to finish her dessert.

It was almost noon the next day before Catherine woke up. She dressed in a hurry as she had arranged to attend the fair's opening ceremony with Paul at 1 p.m. When she was ready she asked the operator to connect her to Room 13. There was a moment's silence; then the operator replied, "But madame, there is no Room 13 in this hotel." Catherine frowned. Had she mistaken the room number?

She went down to the concierge and asked again for Room 13. She got the same reply: "You know, madame, superstition and all that." "Well, what room is my brother in?" "Your brother? But madame arrived alone last evening." The concierge produced the hotel register, which showed Catherine's entry but nothing about Paul.

By this time Catherine had become frantic and called for the manager. Together with him, she went to the first floor. Indeed, there were Rooms 12 and 14, but no 13.

This is supposed to be a true story. Can you figure out what was happening?

What Am I? 7

If you look, you can't see me.
If you see me, you cannot see anything else.
I can make you walk if you can't.
Sometimes I speak the truth.
And sometimes I lie.
If I lie, I am nearer the truth.
What am I?

Rouge et Noir 8

The scene: a famous Monte Carlo casino. A distinguished gentleman with a stunning brunette at his side is playing red or black at the roulette table. Watching them, another couple nearby,

George Benson and Isabelle Labrue, start to talk. "You know, Isabelle, I often wonder why Philip Castle continues to play. He loses most of the time—roughly 500,000 francs a year." "He must be very rich," Isabelle offers. "Not really," responds George. "His wife, Deborah, the lovely creature by his side, is the one with the money and she finances him." "She must be very much in love or very stupid, or she would leave him and find someone with better luck." "On the contrary, she is quite happy with the situation," says George, with a knowing smile. Why?

The Murder   9

It was a busy morning in the city. On a fifth floor terrace of a brownstone in Manhattan, two men were seen to quarrel viciously. A crowd in the street below watched the scene with morbid interest.

Suddenly, one of the men took hold of the other's legs and tossed him over the balustrade. The victim hit the street with a crushing thud and died shortly thereafter. Strangely, it was one of the onlookers, and not the man who had attacked the victim, who was eventually indicted. Why?

The Fifty-Dollar Find 10

A bank manager on his way home from work spotted a $50 banknote lying in the gutter. He picked it up, memorized the number to play in the lottery, and happily pocketed it. When he arrived home, his wife happened to mention that the butcher's bill had arrived and came to exactly $50. With a grin, he produced the found money and she paid the butcher the following day. In turn, the butcher used the $50 banknote to pay the farmer from whom he bought his meat. The farmer then used it to pay his local merchant, who used it to pay his cleaning lady. The cleaning lady used the note to pay her overdraft at the bank.

As it happened, the cleaning lady deposited the banknote at the selfsame bank managed by the man who found it in the first place. Having remembered the number, he now discovered that it was counterfeit! What was lost, if anything, in the whole transaction and by whom?

The Accident 11

On a frosty winter morning, Farmer Jones was walking with his dog through the snow-covered field adjoining his stables. Suddenly, the dog started to bark excitedly, pulling him towards a lonely tree in the middle of the field. It was then that the farmer noticed a man hanging from the tree. The second thing that the observant Jones noticed was that the snow in the field, apart from his and the dog's footprints, was virginal.

The police were called. Forensic examination established that death had occurred some ten hours before and was due to exposure. The field had been snow-covered for more than two days. The police were soon satisfied that the death had been accidental. Explain.

Overheard 12

"I eat what I can and I can what I can't." What does that mean?

The Shopping Mall 13

Herbert Tidy, an efficiency expert, and his wife, Harriet, decided to visit the new shopping mall which had just opened in town. There, Harriet became so involved with the items on display in a hat shop that she didn't notice her husband wasn't with her. When she discovered he wasn't around, her first reaction was to go and look for him; then she remembered what he was always telling her: If two people are trying to find each other, it is more efficient if one stands still than if both search. She was quite happy with this theory as it gave her time to look at more hats until her husband arrived. Despite her recollection of her husband's theory on the efficiency of searches, the strategy was unwise. Suggest why.

Loaded Gun 14

The prosecuting counsel stepped forward and faced the jury. "We are supposed to believe that the defendant, although in possession of a loaded gun at the time of the murder, did not commit the crime—indeed, never even took the weapon out of his pocket." The prosecutor looked across at the defendant with a smug smile on his face. "Yes, the defendant stated at the time of his arrest that the gun had remained, unfired, in the right-hand outside pocket of his overcoat, while an unidentified assailant killed the victim. How is it, then, that when the defendant was searched by the police at the time of the arrest, the gun was found in the inside, left-hand pocket of his overcoat?" (The gun was fully loaded when found, but a cartridge could have been replaced after firing and cleaning the gun.)

As he finished speaking, the prosecutor caught a fleeting look of triumph on the defense counsel's face and felt distinctly uneasy. So he should; the defense produced a completely logical explanation for the movement of the gun although the defendant had not touched it. He was later acquitted. Explain.

Wolf Among the Sheep 15

An old wolf had spent days crossing a vast wasteland without anything to eat. Starving, he came upon a large metal enclosure

in the middle of a field. Inside the compound were many very fat, well-fed sheep. The walls of the enclosure were so high and the bars so close together that it was impossible for the sheep or anything to escape once inside. Due to his long fast, however, the wolf was so thin that he knew he could squeeze in through the bars and feast himself on the sheep to his heart's content. Although hunger urged him on, the wily wolf also realized that, after he ate his fill, he would be unable to escape. The wolf sat and pondered and then found an ingenious solution. What did the wolf do?

The Contract   16

Stephen was about to leave the country but wanted to hand some important documents to his partner, Dave, personally on his way to the airport. When he phoned, Stephen got Dave's answering machine, but knowing that Dave was in the habit of checking for messages at regular intervals he said, "Dave, this is important! I have the Duplex Corporation contract which much be exchanged this afternoon. Please meet me without fail in exactly forty minutes at the corner of 5th Avenue and 55th Street. I can only wait for five minutes, but it's all I need to hand you the papers and give you verbal instructions of a highly confidential nature. Thank you." At that moment the limousine arrived to take Stephen to JFK airport.

The car arrived at the designated corner with three minutes to spare. Stephen had the car wait, confident that Dave would arrive at any moment. After ten minutes, when Dave did not turn up, Stephen was forced to continue to the airport even though an important deal was in jeopardy. Why did Dave, who had, incidentally, heard the message in good time and was not physically prevented, not meet his partner?

Can of Peas   17

A man walked into a shop and asked for a can of peas. "That will be $1 please," said the assistant, handing him the can. The man took the can, looked at it and said, "No, I said peas, not peaches." The assistant took back the can, read the label, and handed it back to the man. "They are definitely peas, sir, look at the label." The man picked up the can, shook it and listened, "No, they are definitely peaches."

The assistant was beginning to get rather angry: "Perhaps you have a vision problem, because the label is quite clear. Even the illustration shows it. The contents are peas." "I'm afraid I do not like your tone of voice," replied the man, "may I, please, see the manager."

The assistant went to get the manager and on their approach the manager, with a condescending smile on his face, asked the man what the problem was. "Your assistant states that the contents of this can are peas but I can assure you they are peaches. He has been very rude to me and I demand that this can be opened to show that I am right, after which an apology is in order."

The can was opened and, sure enough, it contained peaches. The assistant and manager were flabbergasted. The manager offered the man $10 and an abject apology from the assistant. The man accepted the money and the apology and left the shop.

Find an explanation.

Deal a Bridge Hand 18

Andrew Abelson had dealt about half of the cards for a bridge game when he was interrupted by a telephone call. When he returned to the table, no-one could remember where he had dealt the last card. Without counting the number of cards in any of the four partly-dealt hands, or the number of cards yet to be dealt, how could he continue to deal accurately, with everyone getting exactly the same cards he would have had if the deal had not been interrupted?

The Parrot 19

It was now six months since Gertrude James had lost her husband, and living alone with only memories and no-one to talk to had made her very depressed. One day she decided she would get herself a pet to keep her company. After looking around the local pet shop, she could not make up her mind whether to get a dog or a cat. "Why not get a parrot?" the pet-shop manager suggested. *Why not?* she thought, *I could teach it to speak and then I would at least have someone to talk to.*

"Does this parrot speak?" she asked the shopkeeper. "This parrot, madam, will repeat every word it hears, I can assure you," replied the shopkeeper. Gertrude promptly bought the parrot and took it home.

Three months later, after trying almost constantly to get the parrot to speak, Gertrude could not get it to utter one word. Can you come up with an explanation, assuming that the shopkeeper spoke the truth?

Murder in the Family 20

There was a loud knock at the door late one Sunday evening at the home of William and Janet Garner. William answered the door to a man who introduced himself as Detective Greg Nelson of the Los Angeles Police Department and informed William, "I'm afraid that your brother-in-law was found brutally murdered this afternoon." William gasped, "Oh my god! Poor Ben, who could have done such a terrible thing, my wife will be devastated."

William invited Detective Nelson inside and went to awaken his wife, Janet, who had gone to bed early with a headache. When Janet heard the news, she became hysterical, and the doctor was called to administer a sedative. Detective Nelson asked them to come to his office the following morning to make statements.

When William and Janet arrived at police headquarters the following morning, they were shown into Greg Nelson's office. "Have either of you any idea as to who had a motive?" Nelson asked. "It certainly appears that Ben knew his killer."

William looked over at Janet, "There's my sister Elizabeth's husband, Arthur. He's a really weird guy and has threatened Ben during the many arguments they've had." Janet wiped away the tears that were rolling down her cheeks and said quietly, "There's my other brother, Peter, but he and Ben were very close. In any case, Peter is out of town at the moment."

William leaned forward in his seat, "Of course, there is Uncle Lawrence. He always said that Ben wished him dead so that he could get his hands on his money and he was convinced that Ben was trying to kill him. Come to think of it, cousin Philip owed Ben a lot of money, and Ben threatened him with violence if he didn't pay up."

"I've heard enough," interjected Inspector Nelson. "It's obvious to me that you, William Garner, committed the murder and I am placing you under arrest." How did Inspector Nelson come to this conclusion?

The Beach   21

The scene: a deserted beach on a Pacific island. On the shoreline lies an upturned boat with a man lying alongside, attached to it by chains. The man has minor lacerations but is alive. How did he get there?

Smart Kid   22

I have long been an ardent chess player, and my twelve-year-old daughter scarcely knows the moves. Recently, two of my chess-expert friends came to dinner. After eating, I played one game with each of them and lost both games even though against each I had the advantage of a pawn and the opening move.

Just as we finished, my daughter came into the room. On learning of my ill success she said: "Daddy, I'm ashamed of you! I can do better than that. Let me play them. I don't want any advantage: I'll play one game with white pieces and one with black. I'll even give them an advantage by playing both games at once and I'll make out better than you did." And she did! How did she do it?

The Mountain   23

Ali lived in a very beautiful little village nestled in a valley in southern Turkey. An avid mountain-climber, every weekend he climbed the nearby mountain. However, although he was a very proficient climber, he always turned back just before he reached the peak. Why?

The Blind Man 24

A middle-aged man with dark glasses, a guide dog, and a white stick is walking slowly and carefully down the sidewalk of a very busy street in broad daylight. He has perfect eyesight, is not trying to beg, nor has he any criminal intent. What is he doing?

Devoted Couple 25

James and Catherine Barker were an extremely happy and contented couple in their early sixties. Catherine had given up her job to become a full-time housewife when she married James, and he had only twelve months to go before he retired as managing director of a successful engineering company.

James had always been an active man, and his study was crammed with trophies he had won in various sporting activities. He now took great pleasure in cleaning the trophies once a week, and Catherine was happy to let him get on with it. Although James had recently appeared to be rather pale and tired, he assured Catherine that everything was alright.

This Saturday evening, James had settled down in his study for the trophy-polishing ritual, while Catherine watched the 6 p.m. news in the parlor. As the broadcast was ending, Catherine went to the study to ask James if he wanted a cup of tea. She found the study door locked and could hear her husband talking to someone. Wondering how anyone could have arrived without her knowing, she knocked on the door. Suddenly she heard her husband cry out "Put down that knife!" and then a scream.

Catherine became hysterical and ran out into the garden to look through the study window. The study window was open and she could see her husband slumped in his chair with a large knife embedded in his chest. She ran screaming to her neighbors and they immediately phoned the police.

The homicide detectives were very quickly on the scene. James had been stabbed through the heart and had died instantly. There were no fingerprints on the knife nor any sign of a scuffle or evidence that anything had been taken. The chief inspector looked at his colleague and said, "Where's the motive?" His colleague shook his head.

Well, what was the motive?

The Slow Horses

Alexander, the aged and eccentric king of Draconia, decided to abdicate but could not make up his mind which of his two sons should sit on his throne. He finally decided that, as his sons were both accomplished horsemen, he would hold a race in which the loser, i.e. the owner of the slowest rather than the fastest horse, would become king.

Each of the sons owned a superb horse and feared that the other would cheat by holding his own horse back, so they agreed to consult the wisest man in the kingdom. With only two words, the wise man ensured that the race would be fair. What did he say?

Place of Work

Norman Selway has spent five straight days and nights at his place of work, even though there is nothing for him to do there, he was not asked by his employer to stay at his place of work, and he has a perfectly happy homelife. Further, during the last two days he has not eaten or taken a drink, although there is food and water just a few feet away. There are also several restaurants so close that he can see them from where he sits.

Three days ago, his wife rang to tell him that he had won the city lottery and, although they need the money urgently, Norman has done nothing about claiming his prize. The day before, his only son was presented with the Congressional Medal of Honor; John did not attend.

Norman is not sick or suffering from agoraphobia, and he does not have any other physical disability. He can move about freely and he is neither crazy nor on a hunger strike. He is not taking part in any experiment, or trying to win a bet or get his name into the *Guinness Book of Records*. He is completely alone and, oh yes, Norman has a desk job. What is happening?

Last Letter 28

A woman is seated and is writing. There is a thunderstorm outside and she dies as a consequence. How did she die?

A Safe Place 29

Leo Halpern leaves home. When he tries to return, a man wearing a mask blocks his path.

(a) What is Leo doing?
(b) What is the masked man's occupation?
(c) Where is Leo's "safe place"?

The Stranger 30

A married couple was speeding into town when their sedan ran out of gas. The man went for help after making sure his wife closed the windows and locked the doors of the car. Upon his return, he found his wife dead and a stranger in the car. The windows were still closed, the doors were still locked, and no damage was done to the car. How did the woman die, and what was the stranger doing?

The Last Movie   31

Tom and Joe go to a movie. During the picture they exchange angry words. Tom draws a gun, Joe screams, and Tom shoots Joe dead. Tom gets out of his seat and leaves the theater. The shooting and screaming did not coincide with loud noises in the movie soundtrack. Although there were many other people in the theater, no one tried to stop Tom. Why didn't they?

The Careful Driver   32

I'm driving down a highway at the legal 55-miles-per-hour speed limit. I'm sober; my license plates, license, and insurance are in order; and I'm wearing my seat belt. I passed three cars without going over 55 miles per hour, yet a state patrol officer pulled me over and gave me a ticket. Why?

The Phone-In   33

Tom Bradley had left his home in Alperton early that day, to drive to Manchester for a seminar, spread over three days.

As he drove, he switched on the radio and listened to a phone-in program. The moderator was telephoning London subscribers at random to obtain their views on the performance of public transport in the Greater London area. Tom listened to three opinions with slight amusement, nodding in approval when he agreed with a response. Suddenly his face turned angry. He headed towards the next exit and sped for home. Explain.

The Steelworker   34

David Edwin, 45 years old, lives in a high-rise apartment building within walking distance of the local steelworks where he is employed as plant supervisor.

Every morning at 8:00 a.m., he walks down a flight of stairs, and when he arrives at his destination he makes himself a cup of tea. He then reads the morning paper, which he has picked up from the news-vendor at the corner. Halfway through the paper, his eyelids get heavy and he falls asleep for a solid eight hours. Nonetheless, at the end of the month he looks forward to a nice productivity-linked bonus. How does David get away with it?

The Birthday

Alice and George were window shopping in London's Bond Street. As they passed a jeweller, Alice stopped and admired a bracelet, one of three, with the motif of a leopard silhouetted in semi-precious stones. Reading her mind, her husband said, "Darling, I would love to make this your birthday present, but it must be far beyond my budget." "Let's ask, just for fun," ventured Alice, and they entered the shop.

As requested, the sales clerk fetched the leopard bracelet. Alice tried it on and looked pleadingly at her husband. Asked the price, the clerk hesitated for a brief moment and then said, "£250 for payment in cash." George could not hide his surprise, as the piece looked much more costly. "The stones are paste," volunteered the clerk by way of explanation, and he offered to reserve the bracelet until George could return with the cash.

At home, Alice waited impatiently for George and her new bracelet. When he arrived there was a smug smile on his face:

"Darling, you won't believe this, but I showed the bracelet to Oscar, the jeweller in Swiss Cottage, he offered me £800 for it. Now I can buy you all three bracelets!"

When Alice recovered from her shock at this turn of events, she was near tears. "No, George, I have changed my mind. I don't want a bracelet. In fact, I don't want any birthday present at all." Explain.

What Are They? 36

"How much will one cost?" asked the customer in a hardware store. "Twenty cents," replied the clerk. "And how much will twelve cost?" "Forty cents." "Okay. I'll take one hundred and twelve." "Fine. That will be sixty cents." What was the customer buying?

The Keys 37

Andrew Taylor, a fairly successful author of mysteries and thrillers, left his house in Cambridge at 8:00 a.m. to travel to London to see Raymond Berstein, the managing editor of his publishing company, who had expressed his dissatisfaction with the ending of Andrew's latest book.

Andrew had decided that he would go on to Bristol after the meeting to see his ex-wife, with whom he was still on excellent terms, and his two children. He was also looking forward to a couple of days of relaxation.

His meeting with Raymond went very well, and together they had agreed on changes to the ending of the book which improved it tremendously. After his trip to Bristol, Andrew would return to Cambridge refreshed to do the necessary rewrites.

As he was travelling by train to Bristol he suddenly realized that he didn't have his house keys with him. As soon as he arrived he telephoned Raymond and asked him if he had left his keys in his office. "No problem, Andrew old boy, they were on my desk so I have already put them in the mail to you."

Andrew exploded with rage. "You idiot," he said angrily, "how could you do such a stupid thing." Raymond was very hurt by this outburst and could not understand why Andrew was so mad. Can you?

Bank Robbery

The district bank's branch in Coleridge occupied a quaint corner building in the main street. The manager, Richard West, controlled a staff of five. Sets of keys to the premises were kept by the manager, his assistant, and the cleaner.

On the Friday before Christmas, the local traders deposited their week's receipts with the bank, where the money was kept in a somewhat antiquated safe in the manager's office. The safe needed two keys to open it, one held by the manager and one by his assistant.

The bank boasted a primitive burglar alarm which allowed thirty seconds after opening the premises for the alarm to be switched off. For additional protection, a guard was employed to walk around the corner block, which took ten minutes. Whenever the guard passed the manager's office he could satisfy himself, by looking through a peephole, that the door of the safe was intact.

The following Monday morning, the cleaner entered the premises and saw immediately that the safe had been broken into using an acetylene torch. The police were puzzled as the guard assured them that he had walked his rounds as usual and had seen the safe intact until going off duty, just before the cleaner arrived. On the other hand, to crack the safe was a good hour's work. Explain.

The Chairs

Richard Madeley moved back into his family home, a run-down Georgian mansion in Windsor, after the death of his father, being the only remaining member of his family and therefore the sole heir to the estate.

As he had not lived in the house since his parents had divorced when he was a child, he went on a tour of the premises. During the tour, Richard discovered a locked room. He managed to force the door and found among the contents a set of six very beautiful chairs. On inspection Richard guessed that they were probably eighteenth century. The oak frames were in excellent condition but the chairs badly needed upholstering.

The following day, Richard telephoned a local upholsterer to come and look at the chairs. After inspecting them, the upholsterer quoted a price of £200 each for the work. Richard could not afford to have all six chairs re-covered at that price, but decided to have three done, and maybe later, when his finances picked up, the remaining three could be repaired.

Two weeks later, the upholsterer delivered the newly upholstered chairs. They looked exquisite. As Richard paid the upholsterer the sum agreed, the man said, "They look so beautiful, you must have the other three done." "I wish I could, but money is very tight," replied Richard. "Look, I'll make you a deal," responded the upholsterer. "I'll do the other three chairs for half the price of the first three." As Richard considered the offer, the upholsterer seemed to grow agitated. "OK, I'll do them for £50 each."

How could Richard refuse such an offer? He agreed, and the upholsterer immediately loaded the remaining chairs onto his van and drove away. Richard watched the van disappear down the road and suddenly a look of dreadful realization crossed his face. Explain.

Luxury Cruise   40

It is easy to make friends during a transatlantic crossing, but such friendships seldom survive the five days from Southampton to New York.

The following took place during the third evening on the *Queen Mary*. After dinner and a few rounds of bridge, a small but select group gathered for drinks and small talk at the bar on the promenade deck. The group included a real-estate tycoon, Robert Waterman, and his young secretary, Madame Croiseau and her toy-boy, and Count Orlando and his beautiful wife, Elisabeth. Fred Gerrard, the renowned jeweller, was entertaining the party with stories of famous diamonds and their fate.

The great Mogul found in 1650 in India weighed 787 carats in the rough. The Orloff was stolen by a French soldier, bought by Prince Orloff and given to Catherine The Great of Russia. The most famous of them all, the Koh-i-nor, changed hands many times and was acquired by the British in 1849. Possibly the most fascinating story concerned the affair of the diamond necklace, the scandal at the court of Louis XVI in 1785, which discredited the French monarchy and, according to Napoleon, was one of the major causes of the French Revolution.

The conversation then turned to the high cost of insuring precious stones. To solve the problem, jewels were kept in a bank vault and instead replicas were worn by the owners. Waterman was of the opinion that these imitations were of such excellent quality that only the closest expert examination would discover the fake. Fred Gerrard begged to differ and maintained that the trained eye would know the difference at arm's length. This statement was met with disbelief by everyone.

To prove his point, Gerrard looked at Madame Croiseau's diamond bracelet and without hesitation described it as a superb imitation. To alleviate her obvious embarrassment, he added, "Madame, I am sure that the real thing is safe and sound in the ship's vault." A slight nod from madame confirmed his diagnosis. A round of subdued applause acknowledged the expertise.

"On the other hand," he continued, "the Countess's necklace is one of the most exquisite pieces of jewelry I have seen for some time." The Countess visibly blushed and looked at Gerrard with a strange expression. The Count smiled with obvious satisfaction. "This time you are mistaken, dear boy." "Impossible," retorted the jeweller. "Would you care to wager, say $500?" said the Count. Gerrard accepted, and the Countess handed him the necklace for closer examination. He looked at it for a few seconds and then glanced at the Countess. "You win," he said to the Count, handing him the amount wagered. The party broke up and everyone returned to their cabins.

Next morning Gerrard noticed a piece of paper that had been slipped under his cabin door. On it was a lipstick mark and the words "Thank you." Explain.

Day Out   41

The social club in Southville had saved for the whole year to finance an outing to the country fair in Northville, about half an hour away.

On a bright Sunday morning they set out in high spirits, looking forward to an enjoyable day at the fair. Ten minutes later Mr. and Mrs. Jones, prominent members of the club, turned round and headed back towards Southville. Yet after a further twenty minutes they, together with the other club members, arrived at their destination. They did not use any speedier transportation to catch up with their friends. How did they do it?

In the Park   42

It was a warm, sunny day and Jane decided to take three-year-old Sally to the park. When they arrived Jane spread a towel on the ground and watched as Sally played in the grass nearby. Suddenly a large Rottweiler charged across the field straight towards Sally. Instead of panicking, Jane just watched, apparently unconcerned. Why?

Daily Routine   43

Joe leaves his house at 9:00 a.m. sharp every weekday morning, and walks down the block to the corner of a busy street. He stops in front of the general store situated on the corner, then turns and faces the store window with an expectant smile on his face. After a couple of minutes he crosses the road to catch the 9:30 a.m. train to his workplace in the city. Explain.

The Robbers 44

Two robbers break into a jewelry store closed for the weekend and proceed to select the choicest pieces from the display cases. Suddenly one says to the other, "The police are coming, let's take what we have and go." At first the first robber looks mystified as he had neither heard nor seen any evidence that the police were in the vicinity but, turning to the second robber, he looks concerned and says, "OK, let's go." Explain.

Suicide 45

Henry Miller and his wife, Ann, were teaching at the same college. Henry was a philologist and Ann a physicist. They were also joint treasurers and as such had control of the college's funds.

At a recent annual audit it was found that a considerable sum was missing. Henry and Ann were interviewed by the police, then allowed to go home.

The next morning the housekeeper arrived as usual. Finding the door to the bedroom closed and getting no response to her knock, she opened it and discovered their bodies, together with a typed note: "This is the only way out for Ann and I."

The police officers were calling it suicide until one of them shook his head in disagreement. What aroused his suspicion?

Police Emergency 46

The police had been called to a farmhouse twenty miles outside town where they arrested a particularly vicious psychopath who had previously murdered two of the farm's occupants. They were returning to the police station when the prisoner attacked the officer who was sitting with him in the back of the police car. The driver immediately called his station and asked for urgent backup.

The station had only one other car in the vicinity and called it on the radio. The officers, however, did not respond and, as a result, both officers escorting the prisoner were killed and the prisoner escaped. The officers in the second police car were amazed when, upon returning to the station, they were charged with dereliction of duty. Their radio was in perfect working order and yet they had not responded to the emergency call. Why not?

The Lovers 47

Pamela Wells was certainly no shrinking violet; just the opposite. She had three boyfriends on the go at the same time. The whole town, with the exception of the three boyfriends, seemed to know what was going on.

Early one morning, as he gazed at the gentle autumn rain through his office window, Inspector Jones received a call. It was a very distressed Paul Johnson, one of Pamela's boyfriends. He had arrived at her house, an isolated place on the outskirts of town, to find the front door ajar. On entering he had discovered her body; she had been bludgeoned to death. Inspector Jones told Paul to stay at the house, and he and his assistant left immediately for the scene of the crime.

Later that same day, after making extensive enquiries, Inspector Jones assembled his three main suspects, Paul Johnson and the other two boyfriends, Peter Smith and David Brown, at the station to make statements. Peter Smith stated that he had been out of town the previous evening. He had telephoned Pamela at 11:00 p.m. from his hotel and had made arrangements to meet over the weekend. David Brown said that he had been at an office party, gotten quite drunk, and spent the night at a colleague's house. Finally, Paul Johnson pointed out that he had seen Pamela the previous evening. They had had dinner and discussed a planned excursion the following day. He had left at about 9:30 p.m. and returned to his apartment on the other side of town.

Inspector Jones stared hard at Paul. "Mr. Johnson, you are obviously lying about your whereabouts over the last twenty-four hours and I arrest you for the murder of Pamela Wells." How did he know?

The Punctures 48

A train was leaving Paris for the southern coast at the same time as a 200SL Mercedes. The driver of the Mercedes was unaware that both of the front tires had slow punctures, and by the time the car arrived in Lyon those tires were already completely flat. Although the driver did not change or have the tires repaired, the Mercedes reached the French coast at the same time as the train. Explain.

The Banker 49

Gerald Butcher, the London banker, was found dead in his study, slumped over the desk with a gun in his hand and a gunshot through his temple. The blinds were drawn and the desk light was switched on. On top of the desk was a tape recorder. When Inspector Brown pressed the play button he heard Butcher's last message, "I cannot face the disgrace, this is the end . . ." then there was a gunshot. Under the banker's head was a bloodstained letter from the Serious Fraud Office announcing an investigation into Butcher's affairs. It seemed a clear case of suicide and the police were just about to remove the body when Inspector Brown stopped them. "Wait a moment," he said, "this looks like murder." What aroused his suspicion?

The Presidents 50

Bob glanced up from his newspaper, "Here's an unusual story, Tom. It says here that three of the first five presidents of the United States died on July 4th. I wonder what the odds are against a coincidence like that." "I'm not sure," replied Tom, "but I am willing to give ten-to-one odds that I can name one of the three who died on that date."

Assuming that Tom had no prior knowledge of the dates on which any of the presidents died, was he justified in offering such generous odds?

Attica 51

The prisoners were assembled in the mess hall for dinner. Two of the most feared inmates, Jaime Sanchez and Moses Washington, were engaged in a heated discussion about the spiralling violence between their rival factions.

Both men had started their adult life with great promise.

Jaime's parents always thought that their son would follow his father into the medical profession, and had spared no expense to put him through medical school. Things started to go very wrong when Jaime began to take drugs, and very soon he was completely out of control, becoming involved in drug-pushing and eventually murder. Moses, on the other hand, had trained to be a priest but had allowed himself to be influenced by his old friends, who were all members of street gangs. Very soon his religious vocation went out of the window and he became even more vicious and ruthless than the rest of the gang.

Moses glared maliciously across the table at Jaime and called him a vile name. Jaime responded by making crude comments about Moses' parents. Suddenly Moses' face turned purple and he gripped Jaime's arm like a vise. Jaime immediately struck Moses a fearful blow with his fist, then produced from somewhere a vicious-looking handmade knife and stuck it into Moses, who fell forward onto the table bleeding profusely. The guards quickly moved in, and Moses was rushed to the infirmary.

The next day Jaime was brought to visit Moses in the hospital. When Moses saw Jaime he 'took him warmly by the hand, thanked him, and promised that he would never call him names again. Explain.

Eyewitness 52

Claire Vermont, the wealthy widow of the late Raymond Vermont, former publisher of mystery novels, owned a beautiful estate in Westchester. Late one evening she looked through the bay windows of her drawing room and to her horror saw a man strangling a woman.

Claire's first impulse was to open the door and attempt to stop the aggressor. However, she did not. She also did not phone the police although the telephone was in working order. She felt utterly helpless to intervene in spite of the fact that she was not physically constrained in any way. She did not even call out for assistance to the live-in butler, although he was in the house. Explain her strange behavior.

The Galaxy 53

The First National Museum in midtown Manhattan opened the autumn season with a special attraction—the world's third-largest emerald, called the "Galaxy," worth a king's ransom. The stone was placed in the center room of the west wing with the tightest security the museum had ever seen.

Touching the crystal glass dome protecting the stone would trigger audio and optical alarms. Steel shutters would lock all exits within four seconds. The showcase was supervised by closed-circuit television. In other words, robbery was unthinkable.

On opening day, visitors had to line up and were only admitted in groups of forty-five. Among the second group allowed in, one character caused considerable annoyance. He was obviously the worse for drink, staggering from room to room, always lagging behind the others.

The group had just left the center room when all alarms went off. Within five seconds the security guards and a police officer arrived at the scene. The crystal glass dome was shattered and the man was lying on the floor in a drunken stupor. In his left hand he held the Galaxy. The whiskey flask in his right hand was empty.

At the prison hospital, he was found to have an alcohol level five times over the limit. In due course he was given a two-year suspended sentence for willful damage and disorderly conduct. When he left the courtroom he was an extremely happy and richer man. Why?

The Menu   54

A well-dressed couple enters a sumptuous restaurant in midtown Manhattan. They ask for the menu and wine list, which they study intently. They then order cocktails and place their order for a four-course dinner. As they enjoy their drinks, they engage in animated conversation. Suddenly the man looks at his watch and the couple get up and leave hurriedly, without waiting for the meal.

The Maître D' watches them leave, making no attempt to question or stop them. Explain.

A Job in a Million   55

Robert Bradley is a lucky man indeed. He is only twenty-nine and works for an important corporation with offices all over the world. Robert travels extensively, always first class, staying at the best hotels. He does not buy or sell anything and yet is in close contact with important business people and even royalty. When he speaks, everyone listens with undivided attention.

Arriving at his destination, he spends his time at the swimming pool, if he is not out shopping. After a day or two he leaves, without having concluded any business. Explain.

The Thoroughbred   56

Blithe Spirit, ten times winner of the Grand National, is tied to a thirty-foot rope. A haystack is forty feet away. Nevertheless, the horse is able to eat the hay, even though the rope does not break or stretch in any way. How is this possible?

The Crime   57

In some states in the United States a certain crime is punishable, and those who attempt it are usually indicted. However, any perpetrator who is successful is never prosecuted. What is the crime?

Homicide   58

Peter Collins stood accused of murder in the first degree. He pleaded self-defense, claiming he had been attacked by the victim with a kitchen knife. Evidence, one way or the other, was purely circumstantial so, after some hectic plea-bargaining, a guilty plea to manslaughter was accepted and Collins was sentenced to from three to seven years.

In prison, Collins found himself sharing a cell with a contract killer working for the Mafia, who had got away with a two-year sentence for possession of an offensive weapon, a handgun, without a license.

A few months later, when the two men had become friendly, Collins confessed to his cellmate that he had got away with manslaughter but had in fact committed the murder at the request of a crime syndicate. With an air of professional pride, his cellmate, in turn, told Peter in detail about his own several contract killings. Perhaps Peter's syndicate might use the Mafia man's services also when he was released.

Some time later Peter Collins was transferred to another prison. Then a petition by his lawyer to the governor of the state was granted, and Collins was released from prison, having served only five months of his sentence. Explain how.

The Blue Movie 59

Stephen Kelly was leaving a restaurant in London's Soho when he was accosted by a scruffy-looking man, obviously a tout. The following conversation ensued:

Tout: (whispering) Would you like to see a hard-porn blue movie?

Stephen: OK, but how much will you pay me to see it?

Tout: (with some agitation) You don't understand, you have to pay *me* to see it.

Stephen: My good man, it is *you* who do not understand. *You* have to pay me, but I will be reasonable.

Was Stephen joking?

Pools of Water 60

A strange but short-lived phenomenon baffled employees of pubs and clubs in Camden, north London. Pools of water appeared under the cigarette-vending machines. What do you think had happened?

The Phone Rings 61

Eight men were sitting around the boardroom table and one man, armed with a sub-machine gun, was standing at the door. Everyone was silent and the atmosphere was tense. Suddenly the telephone rang. At that moment one of the men jumped up and took a header through the window. Can you find an explanation?

Drink Drive 62

With the festive season approaching, the chief of police ordered a clampdown on drinking and driving. In line with the order, two of his officers were keeping a discreet watch on an exclusive downtown club when they saw a customer stagger out of the door and fall down on the snow-covered ground. After a few seconds he picked himself up, stumbled to his car, and fumbled for the keys. Eventually he got the door open and managed to start the car, grinding the gears before moving off in a zigzag course.

The police car followed, stopped him, and gave him a breathalyser test. The test was negative. Obviously something was wrong

with the equipment, as the man reeked of alcohol. The officers took him to the police station for another test. Again negative. A blood test showed the same result. The police were baffled. Can you solve the mystery?

Peril in the Air I   63

On a scheduled flight from Istanbul to New York an incident occurred which will be remembered by the passengers for a long time. During the flight, a first-class passenger suddenly disappeared from the plane. He did not jump out, nor did anyone push him. In fact, the doors of the plane were closed and secured at the time of the disappearance. Yet his shattered body was discovered elsewhere a few days later. What had happened?

Peril in the Air II   64

Following the sudden disappearance of a passenger, two airline stewardesses, upset as a result of the incident, began to quarrel.

Soon one of them, very distraught, became so agitated that she totally lost control. Running to the door of the plane, she opened it and jumped. She had no parachute (they are not provided on civilian flights); nevertheless, she survived with only a sprained ankle. Was she just incredibly lucky?

The Mask   65

A man doing a dangerous and difficult job has to wear a mask for protection. Suddenly he tears off his mask and as a consequence he dies. He is not under the influence of drugs or alcohol, and does not intend to commit suicide. What makes him tear off his mask?

The Venture   66

Two men decided to embark on a venture which promised to be extremely rewarding financially. They pooled their resources to buy the equipment they needed and, after some extensive promotion, they got under way. Unfortunately, in due course they had to discard some of the material they had bought, in order to save their lives. What were they up to?

The Assassin   67

It was midnight when Joan and Eric arrived home. They had just got out of the car when a man stepped out of shadowy bushes nearby and shot Eric at close range. Eric slumped to the ground. The man fired one more shot, as if to ensure that his victim was dead, and walked away unhurriedly. Joan collapsed in shock and was taken to her house by a neighbor who had heard the shots. She was still under sedation when she was questioned by the police the next morning.

The investigation into the affair had produced evidence of Eric's involvement with organized crime in his early days. Furthermore, Joan was found to be the sole beneficiary of a substantial insurance policy on Eric's life. Her relationship with the neighbor was also unusually close. It was therefore not surprising that Joan was considered a prime suspect.

Furthermore, during questioning, Joan had given a very de-

tailed description of the assassin, which subsequently proved to be completely false. Yes, Joan had deliberately tried to mislead the police, yet neither she nor her neighbor was involved in the homicide. In fact, Joan had been very devoted to her husband. Why, then, did she mislead the police?

The James Dean Appreciation Society   68

The New York chapter of the James Dean Appreciation Society is gathered for the screening of a new Hollywood docudrama based on the life of its members' idol. Just as the movie reaches the point of Dean's untimely death, the audience breaks out into hysterical laughter and applause. Why?

Victoria Station   69

Both Brian and Bill were going from Marble Arch to Victoria Station. Brian was driving at normal speed, while Bill started on foot. Traffic was light, and although Bill ran part of the way and

Brian reached an average speed of 25 miles per hour, both arrived at Victoria Station at the same time. How was this possible?

IRA Justice 70

In Northern Ireland the IRA have a punishment they mete out to petty criminals or informers known as "knee-capping" (firing a single shot into each kneecap).

One night three IRA members entered a "safe" pub where a man was sitting having a drink. They picked him up and frog-marched him out of the pub and into an adjoining field. Without a word being spoken by the IRA members, they shot the man through both knees. As the shots hit, the man screamed loudly and he fell to the ground. Unmoved by the screams of agony, the men turned around, walked quickly back to their car, and sped away.

As the car disappeared into the distance, the man's screams stopped. He got up and walked away. Explain.

The Hundred-Dollar Note 71

Steve was picked up by the police in the drugstore as he was about to pay for his purchase with a hundred-dollar note. Three thousand dollars were found on him, all in $100 bills. He was indicted in connection with the banknotes and for no other crime or felony.

Although it was found that the bills were genuine, not counterfeit, and that Steve could also prove that the money was not stolen or obtained illegally in any way, he received a two-year suspended prison term. Why?

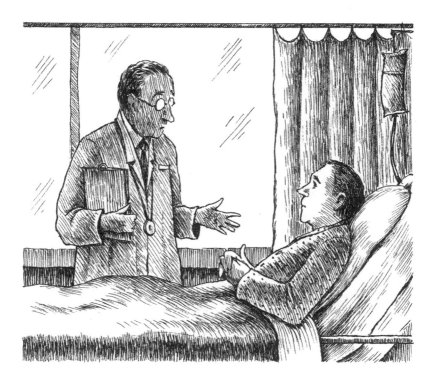

The Operation 72

A man went to the hospital with a suspected malignant tumor in his left kidney. Several tests were made but the results were all negative. Nevertheless, the man insisted on an operation to remove the kidney. Why?

Double Homicide 73

A man discovered that his wife had a lover and there was evidence that they intended to kill him. He decided to preempt their plan, and when, upon returning from a trip, he found them together he killed them both. Realizing that he would be a prime suspect, he had to devise a way to mislead the police. Simply wiping his fingerprints from the murder weapon, a knife, would not help. He managed to produce prints on the knife which would never be traced. How did he do it?

The Judgment 74

A man stood before the judge, charged with killing a long-eared owl, a protected species. Pleading guilty but with extenuating circumstances, the man explained that he had been on a camping trip with his family in a remote region. One day, while they

were all swimming in a nearby lake, their camp caught fire and was completely destroyed, leaving them without shelter or food. After going hungry for two days, they came upon the bird, and he threw a rock that succeeded in killing it. It was cooking and eating the owl, he allowed, that helped them to survive.

The judge, after hearing his story, decided to let the man off. As the man was about to leave the court, the judge called out, "Just as a matter of interest, what does a long-eared owl taste like?" The man paused, thought for a moment, and then answered the judge's question.

The judge then called him back. "On second thought, I retract my earlier decision," he said. "You will pay a fine of $2,000, and consider yourself lucky I do not send you to prison." What did the man say to cause the judge to reverse his original decision?

Discerning Shopper   75

A woman is seen pushing a shopping cart around a large grocery store just before closing time. She stops at various points, carefully selects items and loads them into the cart. When she is finished, she leaves the store. However, she does not pass through the checkout, nor does she pay for any of the items she has selected. Explain.

The Lopsided Coins   76

My friend Carlos is a collector of the paraphernalia which are the working tools of cardsharps, professional con artists, and the like, people who prey on compulsive but unsophisticated gamblers for rich pickings. The items include marked cards, loaded dice, and coins which have a bias towards heads or tails.

It was the latter which was the subject of animated discussion between Carlos and myself. We wondered whether, in full knowledge of the bias, we could use the coins for a game of "heads or tails" which would be fair to both players. There are two coins involved, one biased towards heads and the other, precisely to the same degree, towards tails. Can you suggest a procedure which would give two gamblers an equal chance on flipping the coins?

The Slimming Pill 77

After ten years of intensive research, Dr. Wertheimer of Johns Hopkins developed a slimming pill which was safe, had no side-effects, and did not involve dieting of any sort. He demonstrated the effectiveness of the pill with a test group of forty volunteers who took a pill twice daily, after lunch and dinner, for a period of five weeks.

When the results were logged, it transpired that the average weight loss of ten pounds enjoyed by some participants in the test was almost precisely balanced by a weight gain suffered by the rest of the group. Why?

Pilot Error 78

Tim Shaw, a pilot for eighteen years, had an outstanding safety record. One afternoon he was trying to land a British Airways 747. Visibility was good in spite of a slight snow flurry. He was easing the plane gently down towards the runway when it happened. It appeared that Tim had throttled back too early and the Jumbo jet, one of the safest planes in service, stalled and crash-landed.

Although no one was hurt, the accident was clearly due to pilot error, yet Tim Shaw was not grounded. He continued flying and, in spite of this blemish on his record, his career remained unaffected. How was this possible, considering the stringent safety measures applied by all international airlines?

The Kangaroo Court 79

During the 1950s and '60s a terrorist group active in Germany was trying to destabilize the ruling establishment. One cell, consisting of a young woman and five men, kidnapped a junior official of the Ministry of the Interior. They held a mock trial, accusing him of being responsible for brutal police tactics, and duly sentenced him to death. One of the terrorists, Hans Helldorf, who had particularly suffered from police brutality, volunteered to carry out the execution. He shot the official three times quickly at close range, stepping back to avoid the blood as the man pitched forward. Hans then reached down to check the

man's pulse, nodded with satisfaction, and the group departed hurriedly.

The terrorist murder made the headlines the next morning in all the papers. A few days later Helldorf met a high-ranking police officer in plainclothes and confessed. The policeman made notes, shook hands with Helldorf, and departed. Explain.

The Suspect   80

Clifford Bradshaw, the banker, was found stabbed to death by his live-in housekeeper one Sunday morning. The prime suspect was his nephew, Brian, who was Clifford's sole heir. According to the housekeeper, the two had often quarrelled, sometimes virulently, and yet they were dependent on each other emotionally, having no other living relatives.

Brian was in the habit of visiting Clifford regularly after work, about 5:00 p.m. On the Saturday evening before Clifford's death,

Brian had come for dinner and had left at about 11:00 p.m. No fingerprints could be found on the knife except Clifford's. The housekeeper, who disliked Brian intensely, told the police that Brian was the last to see Clifford alive, and obviously had a strong motive as Clifford had been considering changing his will in her favor. However, under close questioning the housekeeper had to admit that she had been in her room when Brian had left and that she had heard the two arguing in the corridor as the clock chimed the hour. She had then heard Clifford's study door slam and through the window she had seen Brian leave the house, step into his chauffeured limousine and be driven off.

She also had to admit that it was impossible for Brian to have returned without her knowing. Furthermore, Brian had a foolproof alibi, having spent the rest of the night with friends playing poker. The postmortem established the time of death that night at between 10:30 and 12:30.

In view of the circumstances, the housekeeper became the obvious suspect, although without the will change she did not seem to have had a motive. Suicide was a possibility, but unlikely. In fact, as was later established, Brian had committed the murder. How? When the housekeeper later went over her statement she suddenly realized the fatal flaw in Brian's plan. What was it?

The System   81

Two men, Frank and Johnny, were walking from the Hotel de Paris in Monte Carlo to the Winter Casino just a few steps away. Frank, wearing his tuxedo, walked straight in while Johnny, in a plain dark suit, lingered outside for a few minutes before going into the *Salle Privée*. Johnny took a seat at the roulette table opposite Frank but ignored him, as if they were strangers, then both men started to gamble heavily, but only on *chances simples*. If Frank bet on red, Johnny bet the same amount on black. The same with *pair* and *impair*, and so on.

It so happened that another Hotel de Paris guest who knew them watched the two gamblers. After a little while he turned to his wife: "Look at what Frank and Johnny are doing. Doesn't seem like much of a system. They can't win but will lose every time zero comes up." What do you think was going on?

Secrets of the Lake   82

Until she decided to take her husband's tuxedo to the cleaners, Madelaine was at peace with the world. She had it all: a beautiful house bordering Lake Léman, near Geneva, and a handsome husband, René, who had an executive position with Banque Romande at a substantial salary. Madelaine herself was a partner in the law firm of Déverin-Millefleurs in Lausanne. The couple had two lovely children, twins, a boy and a girl ten years old. But when Madelaine emptied the pockets of the tuxedo, she found a torrid love letter written by her best friend, Desirée. Her world collapsed and for days she struggled with the torture of the knowledge and whether or not she should confront René.

One late afternoon she took the children on a motorboat ride on the lake. Two hours later she returned alone, completely distraught and in a state of severe shock. Questioned by the police, she told the story of a catastrophic outing. The children had tried to retrieve something they had seen floating in the lake and had fallen overboard. Madelaine had been unable to save them.

The story made little sense to the police, particularly as Madelaine was known as a good swimmer. Also, since her clothes were dry, she had obviously not made a serious attempt to rescue the twins. The terrible suspicion hardened when, on searching the home, the police found Desirée's letter.

After several hours of intensive interrogation, Madelaine couldn't hold out any longer and made a full confession. However, after studying the case, the *Juge d'Instruction* decided not to proceed and Madelaine was released without charge. Explain.

The Vandal   83

A rough-looking stranger enters a restaurant with a sledgehammer. He selects one of two identical pieces of equipment and, without warning, smashes it into fragments. He then walks out without uttering a word.

The restaurant owner is not surprised. In fact, he seems to have expected the visit and makes no attempt to interfere. However, after the visitor leaves, the owner makes one telephone call, as a result of which the body of the stranger is discovered next morning in a ditch outside town. What has happened?

Walking to the Park   84

Eric Black left his apartment in New York each morning at precisely 8:00 a.m. for his daily walk in Central Park. Passersby smiled as he walked down the street because his walk, with its strange, exaggerated steps, resembled something straight out of the "Ministry of Silly Walks" from the Monty Python shows. However, as soon as he arrived at the park his walk became perfectly normal. Explain.

Nelson's Column

Rudolf Mueller from Dusseldorf arrived in London on his first trip abroad. He wanted to see as much as a four-day stay would permit. He was particularly interested in famous sights, including the Tower of London, Madame Tussaud's, Trafalgar Square, and Nelson's Column. Needless to say, he included Buckingham Palace and the Changing of the Guards.

Back at his hotel in Sussex Gardens, he studied all the tourist pamphlets to acquaint himself with the historical background. He read that the Tower of London was built in 1078 and that Nelson's Column was erected to celebrate the famous victory at Trafalgar, and that it was 170 feet high. This meant nothing to Rudolf as he was used to the metric system. Remembering from his school days that three feet equalled one yard, and that one yard was approximately equal to one metre, he pencilled in, next to a photograph of the column, 56½ metres. Sadly, his inaccurate calculation cost the life of his best friend. Explain.

Witnesses for the Defense 86

Bruce and Harry had planned the bank holdup with the greatest care. The victim was a suburban branch of the First State Bank on a Friday afternoon, one minute before closing. All the cash from the local shops would be there for the weekend, and if the robbers locked the doors behind them as they entered the bank, no one would be surprised.

The raid went precisely as planned. There was no resistance from the staff, the automatics saw to that—and the haul exceeded their expectations. After the staff was bound and gagged, the robbers left the premises unhurriedly. The video cameras, however, had done their work well, and the police had no problem identifying the culprits, who had worn no disguises, within hours. They were caught the next day.

Although Bruce and Harry denied strenuously being the robbers, every one of the bank's staff identified them, picking them out of police lineups, so it looked like an open-and-shut case. The prosecution relied on the video films and the testimony of the bank's staff. The defense called only two witnesses, but as a result the judge had to direct the jury to find the defendants not guilty. How do you explain this extraordinary turn of events?

Foreign Exchange 87

One of the breakaway republics from the former Soviet Union needed new banknotes with a high denomination to cope with inflation. Their newly formed central bank approached a British company specializing in the printing of banknotes for foreign governments. After some haggling about the cost, a purchase order was issued and an artist's drawing of the design was sent by special courier to the London printer.

The printers, using advanced photographic technology, produced two sets of master plates and printed one million banknotes under the customary strict-security measures. When the print run was completed, they dispatched one set of master plates, the notes, and an invoice to their customer.

A few days later, the printer in London received a strongly worded fax from their customer, refusing to pay and threatening litigation as the banknotes received were completely useless. The new notes were obviously an exact replica of the artist's drawing and the paper used was in accordance with the specifications. What went wrong?

After considering the fax for a little while, the printer, who was a member of Mensa with an IQ of 161, sent a fax in reply, whereupon he was visited by the country's ambassador, who first apologized and then thanked him profusely. He handed the printer a banker's draft for the full amount of the invoice plus a bonus of fifty percent. Can you explain this extraordinary turn-about?

The Hijack   88

Shortly after 11:00 a.m. one October morning, two men were busy unloading a shipment of dresses in Manhattan's garment district. Just as they opened the back door of their delivery truck, three men approached them, one brandishing an Uzi subma-

chine gun, forced them back into the truck, handcuffed them, and locked them in.

No one passing by noticed the incident to report it to the police, nor did the police have any prior information of the planned hijack. Nevertheless, two 5th Precinct officers were on the lookout for the truck as it approached the entrance to the Manhattan Bridge and after spotting it they took up a pursuit that ended when the raiders crashed in Brooklyn. Assuming that the police had no other reason to stop or pursue the vehicle, how do you account for their remarkable success in apprehending the hijackers?

The Orchard   89

Bob Wilson was very partial to fresh fruit, and therefore had his own little orchard so that he could pick whatever fruit he desired straight from the tree: cherries, apples, apricots, he had them all, and more.

One afternoon he fancied a few cherries, but as he was picking them he fell and, although he was not climbing the tree, Bob was killed almost instantly from multiple fractures. Explain.

The Vacancy   90

Frank Kolmin was president of United Technologies, a multi-national company with offices spanning the globe. The head-quarters, in New York's Empire State Building, occupied floors 12 through 15, but Frank was a roving ambassador for the group, visiting South America, Europe, and the Far East regularly.

One day he placed the following advertisement in the *Wall Street Journal*:

"Part-time sales rep required for occasional overseas travel. No previous experience necessary, but working knowledge of French and Urdu are a condition. Excellent salary and commission. Suitable candidates may write, enclosing CV, to *Wall Street Journal*, Box #82."

Kolmin had no need for an applicant fitting that description. Why, then, did he advertise?

CLUES

SECTION A

Dusk or Dawn 1

Q Was Norman completely disoriented as to time?
A Yes.

Spring in the Mountains 2

Q Is the season of the year important?
A Yes.

Winter Time 3

Q Were all clocks in good working order when reset?
A Yes.

The Explorers 4

Q Was their base far away?
A No.

Avoiding the Train 5

Q Could the man have run less than 10 feet and still avoid the train?
A No.

The Paris Fair 6

Q Did the operator and the concierge tell the truth?
A No.

Q Were they instructed by someone to mislead Catherine?
A Yes.

Wolf Among the Sheep 15

Q Was the wolf's willpower stronger than his hunger?
A Yes.

The Contract 16

Q Did Dave want the deal to go through?
A Yes.

Can of Peas 17

Q Can one recognize the contents of a tin by shaking it?
A No.

Deal a Bridge Hand 18

Q Would the system work irrespective of the number of cards already dealt?
A Yes.

The Parrot 19

Q Was the shopkeeper honest?
A No.

Murder in the Family 20

Q Did Inspector Nelson have any clues as to the culprit before he spoke to the Garners?
A No.

The Beach 21

Q Was the man heading for the island on which he was stranded?
A Yes.

Q Was he alone in the boat when he started the journey?
A No.

Smart Kid 22

Q Did she win both games?
A No.

The Mountain   23

Q Was there any physical impediment?
A No.

The Blind Man   24

Q Does the man always pretend to be blind?
A No.

Devoted Couple   25

Q Did James have any enemies who might want him dead?
A No.

The Slow Horses   26

Q Did the sons interfere in any way with the horses to affect their running speeds?
A No.

Place of Work   27

Q Could Norman have gone home had he wanted to?
A No.

Last Letter   28

Q Was she writing at a desk or table?
A No.

A Safe Place   29

Q Does this happen to Leo frequently?
A Yes.

The Stranger   30

Q Was the woman murdered?
A No.

The Last Movie   31

Q Could Tom have been stopped?
A Yes.

The Careful Driver 32

Q Was there anything wrong with the car?
A No.

The Phone-In 33

Q Did he hear something on the radio which affected him personally?
A Yes.

The Steelworker 34

Q Is David's boss concerned about his conduct?
A No.

The Birthday 35

Q Was it Alice's idea to go window shopping?
A Yes.

What Are They? 36

Q Could the customer have used fewer than one hundred and twelve?
A No.

The Keys 37

Q Did Raymond mail the correct keys?
A Yes.

Bank Robbery 38

Q Was there enough time for the safe to be cracked between the guard's last round and the arrival of the cleaners?
A No.

Q Did the guard perform his duty correctly?
A Yes.

The Chairs 39

Q Was the upholsterer acting in good faith?
A No.

Luxury Cruise 40

Q Was Gerrard really the expert he pretended to be?
A Yes.

Q Had he known the Countess before the cruise?
A No.

Q Did Gerrard believe that the necklace was genuine?
A Yes.

Day Out 41

Q Had the Joneses forgotten something in Southville?
A No.

In the Park 42

Q Was there something wrong with Jane's vision?
A No.

Daily Routine 43

Q Would Joe ever cross the road without waiting?
A No.

The Robbers 44

Q Did the robber who warned his accomplice have access to special knowledge?
A Yes.

Suicide 45

Q Did the Millers really misappropriate the college's funds?
A No.

Police Emergency   46

Q Was there anything wrong with the backup car's radio?
A No.

The Lovers   47

Q Was there anything in Paul's statement which could not be
reconciled with evidence at the scene of the crime?
A Yes.

The Punctures   48

Q Did the train experience unscheduled delays?
A No.

The Banker   49

Q Did Butcher's wife recognize her husband's voice in the
taped message?
A No.

The Presidents   50

Q Did Tom know the names of some of the U.S. presidents?
A Yes.

Attica   51

Q Was Jaime punished for his deed?
A No.

Eyewitness   52

Q Did Claire know the murderer?
A Yes.

The Galaxy   53

Q Was the culprit drunk when he entered the museum?
A No.

The Menu 54

Q Were the couple hungry when they entered the restaurant?
A No.

A Job in a Million 55

Q Is Robert travelling in company?
A Yes, invariably.

The Thoroughbred 56

Q Is the rope in one piece?
A Yes.

The Crime 57

Q Is the crime committed fairly frequently?
A Yes.

Homicide 58

Q Did Peter Collins have any connection with a crime syndicate?
A No.

The Blue Movie 59

Q Was Stephen serious about wanting to be paid?
A Yes.

Pools of Water 60

Q Was somebody's action responsible for the pools of water?
A Yes.

The Phone Rings 61

Q Were the eight men part of a group with a common purpose?
A Yes.

Drink Drive   62

Q Was the man just a practical joker?
A No.

Peril in the Air I   63

Q Was it an accident?
A Yes.

Peril in the Air II   64

Q Was the stewardess who jumped held responsible for the first
incident?
A No.

The Mask   65

Q Could he do his job without the mask, even if at some risk?
A No.

The Venture   66

Q Was the discarded material expensive?
A No.

The Assassin   67

Q Did Joan anticipate the assassination?
A No.

The James Dean Appreciation Society   68

Q Was the hysterical laughter a reaction to a scene in the
docudrama?
A No.

Victoria Station   69

Q Did Bill use a taxi to catch up with Brian?
A No.

IRA Justice   70

Q   Did the IRA use real bullets?
A   Yes.

The Hundred-Dollar Note   71

Q   Was it likely that a teller would have accepted the notes?
A   No.

The Operation   72

Q   Did the man instruct the surgeon which kidney was to be removed?
A   No.

Double Homicide   73

Q   Is the husband's profession a clue to the mystery?
A   Yes.

The Judgment   74

Q   Was the man in contempt of court?
A   No.

Discerning Shopper   75

Q   Has she found a way to evade the checkout?
A   No.

The Lopsided Coins   76

Q   Are there several ways in which the bias could be eliminated?
A   Yes.

The Slimming Pill   77

Q   Did Dr. Wertheimer adopt standard testing procedures?
A   Yes.

Pilot Error 78

Q Was Tim familiar with piloting a 747?
A No.

The Kangaroo Court 79

Q Was there positive identification of the corpse?
A No.

The Suspect 80

Q Did the housekeeper at first overlook a vital clue?
A Yes.

The System 81

Q Was it important to their scheme to pretend that they did not know each other?
A Yes.

Secrets of the Lake 82

Q Were the events accidental?
A No.

The Vandal 83

Q Did the restaurant owner know the motive of the stranger?
A Yes.

Walking to the Park 84

Q Was Eric behaving normally when he felt observed?
A Yes.

Nelson's Column 85

Q Did Rudolf convert the measurement into metric for a purpose?
A Yes.

Witnesses for the Defense 86

Q   Were the robbers aware of the video cameras?
A   Yes.

Foreign Exchange 87

Q   Were the notes put into regular circulation?
A   No.

The Hijack 88

Q   Did the police know the registration number and color of the truck?
A   Yes.

The Orchard 89

Q   Did Bob just trip unluckily?
A   No.

The Vacancy 90

Q   Did Frank receive several applications?
A   Yes.

SECTION B

Dusk or Dawn   **1**

Q Did Norman know in which direction the Amazon flows?
A Yes.

Spring in the Mountains   **2**

Q Is St. Anton popular for winter sports?
A Yes.

Winter Time   **3**

Q Did the two clocks show the same wrong time?
A Yes.

The Explorers   **4**

Q Could the base protect the field workers?
A No.

Avoiding the Train   **5**

Q Was the train steam-powered?
A Yes.

Q Did the train's whistle blow just before the man started to run?
A Yes.

The Paris Fair   **6**

Q Did the organizer of the fair participate in the charade?
A Yes.

Q Was Paul relocated for his and other people's safety?
A Yes.

What Am I?   **7**

Q Is it something that happens at specific times?
A Yes.

Rouge et Noir 8

Q Do the Castles really lose over the years?
A Yes, but only about one-seventieth of what Philip loses.

The Murder 9

Q Was the man indicted in this case guilty of something less than murder?
A Yes, negligence.

The Fifty-Dollar Find 10

Q Was the bank manager an honest man?
A Yes.

The Accident 11

Q Did the man die of natural causes?
A Yes.

Overheard 12

Q Does the speaker do something with food?
A Yes.

The Shopping Mall 13

Q Would the strategy have been sound if an additional stratagem had been agreed?
A Yes.

Loaded Gun 14

Q Was the overcoat appropriate to the weather?
A Yes, it had started to rain.

Wolf Among the Sheep 15

Q Did the wolf's strategy give him all the meat he wanted to eat?
A Yes.

The Contract   16

Q Was Dave confused by Stephen's message?
A Yes.

Can of Peas   17

Q What was the date of the intended purchase?
A The first of April.

Deal a Bridge Hand   18

Q Does Andrew, on returning to the table, deal differently from when he left?
A Yes.

The Parrot   19

Q Was the shopkeeper's statement a lie?
A No.

Q Was something wrong with the parrot?
A Yes.

Murder in the Family   20

Q Did William Garner give himself away by what he said?
A Yes.

The Beach   21

Q Was the handcuffed man a prisoner of the men who had been accompanying him?
A Yes.

Smart Kid   22

Q Did she play better than either of her opponents?
A No.

The Mountain   23

Q   Could Ali have reached the peak of the mountain if he had really wanted to?
A   Yes, with some inconvenience.

The Blind Man   24

Q   Is he being paid for what he is doing?
A   Yes.

Devoted Couple   25

Q   Was James hiding something from his wife?
A   Yes.

Place of Work   26

Q   Was his life in danger?
A   Eventually, yes.

The Slow Horses   27

Q   Did the two sons ride the horses as fast as they could go?
A   Yes.

Last Letter   28

Q   Was she doing her job when writing?
A   Yes.

A Safe Place   29

Q   Does Leo enjoy the experience?
A   Yes.

The Stranger   30

Q   Did the stranger explain what had happened?
A   No.

The Last Movie   **31**

Q Did anybody hear the shooting?
A No.

The Careful Driver   **32**

Q Were the cars I passed upset about it?
A Yes.

The Phone-In   **33**

Q Did the moderator ring Tom's home phone number?
A Yes.

The Steelworker   **34**

Q Does David's conduct affect his productivity?
A No.

The Birthday   **35**

Q Had Alice seen the bracelet before?
Λ Yes.

What Are They?   **36**

Q Did the one hundred and twelve cost only three times as
much to produce as the one?
A Yes.

The Keys   **37**

Q Did the keys arrive before Andrew returned home?
A Yes.

Bank Robbery   **38**

Q Was there any sign of forced entry into the bank premises?
A No.

The Chairs 39

Q Would £50 per chair have covered the cost to the upholsterer for the repair?
A No.

Luxury Cruise 40

Q Was the necklace genuine?
A Yes.

Q Did the Countess know that it was genuine?
A Yes.

Q Did the Count know?
A No.

Day Out 41

Q Did the social club travel by public transport?
A Yes.

In the Park 42

Q Was Sally afraid of the approaching Rottweiler?
A No.

Daily Routine 43

Q Is Joe waiting for a reason?
A Yes.

The Robbers 44

Q Did the robber who voiced the warning simply have a hunch?
A No.

Suicide 45

Q Was it Henry's profession which caused the police officer to doubt it was suicide?
A Yes.

Police Emergency 46

Q Did the police officers in the backup car receive the message?
A No.

The Lovers 47

Q Was the fact that Paul travelled by car the key to solving the murder?
A Yes.

The Punctures 48

Q If the driver had noticed the punctures during the trip, could he have done anything about them?
A No.

The Banker 49

Q Was there anything in the message which aroused Brown's suspicion?
A Yes.

The Presidents 50

Q Did Tom know the name of the last U.S. president to die on the 4th of July?
A Yes.

Attica 51

Q Does Jaime's medical training have anything to do with the surprising outcome?
A Yes.

Eyewitness 52

Q Was Claire prevented from using the phone in her home?
A Yes.

The Galaxy 53

Q Was the incident planned?
A Yes.

The Menu 54

Q Did the couple plan to leave after placing their order?
A Yes.

A Job in a Million 55

Q Does Robert do any part of his work while he is travelling?
A Yes.

The Thoroughbred 56

Q Was the rope securely fastened to the horse?
A Yes.

The Crime 57

Q Does the crime generally present any danger to third parties?
A No.

Homicide 58

Q Did Peter in fact commit the murder?
A No.

The Blue Movie 59

Q Has Stephen been paid before for watching a movie?
A Yes.

Pools of Water 60

Q Was the water evidence of a crime?
A Yes.

The Phone Rings 61

Q Did the man who jumped through the window fear for his life?
A Yes.

Drink Drive 62

Q Did the "drunken" man act in concert with others?
A Yes.

Peril in the Air I 63

Q Was the disappearance of the passenger noted by some of the passengers as well?
A Yes.

Peril in the Air II 64

Q Did the stewardess realize where she was before she jumped?
A Yes.

The Mask 65

Q Is the worker in full control of his faculties when he tears off his mask?
A No.

The Venture 66

Q Was the discarded material used for the purpose for which it was intended?
A Yes.

The Assassin 67

Q Did Joan know the assassin?
A No.

The James Dean Appreciation Society 68

Q Was the fan club travelling when the incident happened?
A Yes.

Victoria Station 69

Q Did Bill and Brian arrive precisely at the same time?
A Yes.

IRA Justice 70

Q Did the man who was shot wear any protective material?
A No.

The Hundred-Dollar Note 71

Q If Steve could have passed the bills, would he have made a profit?
A Yes.

The Operation 72

Q Was there an alternative to the removal of the kidney?
A Yes.

Double Homicide 73

Q Were the fingerprints from someone known personally to the husband?
A No.

The Judgment 74

Q Was the man's reply evidence of another felony?
A Yes.

Discerning Shopper 75

Q Was she noticed by the store's staff?
A Yes.

The Lopsided Coins 76

Q Does one method to exclude bias involve flipping both coins at the same time?
A Yes.

The Slimming Pill 77

Q Were the numbers of losers and gainers approximately the same?
A Yes.

Pilot Error 78

Q Was the plane damaged?
A No.

The Kangaroo Court 79

Q Was the group responsible for the assassination apprehended?
A Yes.

The Suspect 80

Q Was the murder committed at about 11:00 p.m.?
A Yes.

The System 81

Q Was the loss due to zero outweighed by an advantage?
A Yes.

Secrets of the Lake 82

Q Did René forgive Madelaine when he heard the full story?
A Yes.

The Vandal 83

Q Could the tough-looking stranger have demolished the other piece of equipment to equal effect?
A No.

Walking to the Park 84

Q Was Eric's walk normal as he crossed the street from one pavement to another?
A Yes.

Nelson's Column   85

Q   Did Rudolf's friend visit London?
A   Yes.

Witnesses for the Defense   86

Q   Did the robbers deliberately wear no disguises?
A   Yes.

Foreign Exchange   87

Q   Were the banknotes eventually disposed of?
A   Yes.

The Hijack   88

Q   Did the police receive information about the truck and the
hijack from someone on the scene?
A   Yes.

The Orchard   89

Q   Could the accident have happened without picking any fruit?
A   Yes.

The Vacancy   90

Q   Did Frank know the successful applicant?
A   Yes.

SOLUTIONS

Dusk or Dawn   1

Andrew knew, of course, that the Amazon flows from west to east. It is also obvious that the sky at dawn is lighter in the east, and gradually darker towards the west, while at dusk the reverse is the case.

If he had had a watch he would have known instantly, as in the Brazilian winter (summer in the northern hemisphere) the sun rises early in the morning and sets late in the evening.

Spring in the Mountains   2

The couple had been walking in the mountains during the winter when they were hit by an avalanche and buried. In the spring, when the snow melted, their bodies were exposed.

Winter Time   3

Eight clocks ran on house electricity. During the night there was a power cut, or outage, which affected these clocks but not the other two, which were wound up or battery-operated.

The Explorers   4

The two men were deep-sea diving to explore the ocean floor for valuable minerals. They were diving to a depth of 100 metres, at which depth air in its natural proportion becomes dangerous.

During resurfacing, nitrogen bubbles can form in the diver's circulation (the bends), causing fatal blockages. To allow for safe decompression, the time for re-ascent can take hours. Several pioneers, including Arne Zetterstrom of Sweden, lost their lives by ascending too quickly.

Avoiding the Train   5

The man was walking through a train tunnel and was almost at the end when he heard a whistle and spotted the train coming towards him. He therefore had to move forward, towards the train, so that he could jump clear safely.

The Paris Fair 6

Paul had been taken ill during the night and it was discovered that he had typhoid. So as not to cause panic and jeopardize the World's Fair, the hotel management had arranged for Paul to be taken to an isolation hospital run by nuns and had sealed Room 13 to conceal the fact that Paul had ever arrived. (A true story, and the subject of a book and a movie.)

What Am I? 7

A dream.

Rouge et Noir 8

Each time Philip bets 500 francs on red, Deborah places 500 francs on black. Because of zero, they lose their stake about once in every seventy-four throws, but Deborah accepts this modest loss. The activity keeps her husband happy and they both enjoy the exciting ambiance of the casino.

The Murder 9

They were filming a scene from a thriller and one of the two men on the terrace was a stuntman. When he was thrown from the building he was supposed to fall into a safety net. The man in charge of the safety net had not rigged it properly, however, and the stuntman had fallen to his death. The man responsible for safety on the picture was charged with gross negligence.

The Fifty-Dollar Find 10

Since the same counterfeit note was used in all transactions, they are all invalid. But, realizing what had happened, the bank manager simply reimbursed the bank, saving the cleaning lady from being the sole loser. The manager did not really lose, as he had good value from the butcher, but the $50 *find* was wiped out.

The Accident 11

The man had parachuted from a plane and become entangled in the tree.

Overheard 12

The operative word is "can," as in "tin can," and the solution is therefore self-evident.

The Shopping Mall 13

Herbert was following his own theory, and was waiting for Harriet in the bookshop. His general strategy needs to be improved by identifying who should stay put.

Loaded Gun 14

The defendant was in fact not guilty. As stated, he had put the gun in the right-hand pocket of his overcoat. It was a reversible coat, however, and when it started to rain, he reversed the coat, thereby switching the gun from outside right to inside left.

Wolf Among the Sheep 15

The wolf squeezed through the bars, killed as many sheep as he thought necessary, tore them into small pieces and pushed them through the bars, followed through and ate his fill at leisure outside the compound. Some time later, in a Mensa IQ test, the wolf scored 161.

The Contract 16

When Stephen telephoned Dave's answering machine he forgot to say what time it was when he phoned, making it impossible for Dave to know from what time the "40 minutes" started.

Can of Peas 17

The man was an inveterate practical joker and had a can of peaches in his bag with an identical label to the peas can, which he had switched after a previous purchase. When the assistant went to get the manager, the man replaced the genuine can of peas with the fake can.

Deal a Bridge Hand 18

Andrew dealt the bottom card to himself, then continued dealing from the bottom counterclockwise.

The Parrot 19

The parrot was deaf.

Murder in the Family 20

William Garner knew right away which of his brothers-in-law had been murdered. Inspector Nelson had never specified which one was dead.

The Beach 21

The island was the infamous Devil's Island. The man was a prisoner being rowed ashore by two prison guards. The main prison ship could only moor a quarter of a mile offshore because of treacherous reefs. During the journey the boat had been hit by a sudden squall and both guards had been thrown overboard and drowned, whereas the prisoner, who was chained to the boat, had survived when the boat turned over, trapping an air pocket.

Smart Kid 22

Let us call the experts Mr. White and Mr. Black, according to the color of the pieces each played against my daughter. Mr. White played first. My daughter copied his first move as her opening against Mr. Black at the other board. When Mr. Black answered this move, she copied his move at the first board as her reply to Mr. White, and so on. In this way the simultaneous games against the two experts became a single game between them; my daughter served as a messenger to transmit the moves.

Hence she was certain to either win one game and lose the other or draw both, bettering my showing.

The Mountain 23

The border between Turkey and Iraq runs across the mountain, with the peak being on the Iraqi side.

The Blind Man 24

He is an actor rehearsing a scene for the starring role in a TV series about a blind detective.

Devoted Couple 25

James knew that he was suffering from a terminal illness, and had decided to commit suicide, firstly to spare his wife having to look after him as his illness became worse, and secondly so that she would receive full insurance to provide for her needs. He therefore staged his own murder as the insurance policy had a suicide-exclusion clause. He had locked the study door, opened the window, started a conversation with an imaginary visitor as soon as he heard his wife try the door handle, and then he had stabbed himself, using the cloth which he had been using to clean his trophies to keep the knife clear of fingerprints. The cloth had fallen to the floor after he stabbed himself.

The Slow Horses 26

Switch horses!

Place of Work 27

Norman is the navigator on a naval submarine which has sunk in shallow waters a half mile out of port, on what was supposed to be a one-day test run. All rescue attempts have so far failed, as the escape hatch had jammed. He is alone, being the last surviving crew member, the others having drowned due to a leak. The food and water close at hand are fish and the sea. He can see the shore and several seafront restaurants through the periscope by which he is sitting.

Last Letter   28

She was a skywriter. Lightning struck her plane and she crashed.

A Safe Place   29

(a) Playing baseball.
(b) Catcher.
(c) Third base.

The Stranger   30

The woman died during childbirth. The stranger in the car was the baby.

The Last Movie   31

They were at a drive-in movie.

The Careful Driver   32

I was travelling in the wrong direction down a one-way street; the cars I passed were all going the other way.

The Phone-In   33

The moderator had just announced, "We are now contacting Mr. and Mrs. Bradley of Alperton for their views." Tom heard the ringing tone and, much to his surprise, a man answered the phone. Tom recognized the voice as that of his friend Michael, whom he had suspected of having an affair with his wife.

The Steelworker   34

David Edwin works the night shift at the steelworks and, as he lives in the basement of the high-rise, has to descend the stairs to reach his apartment.

The Birthday   35

Alice had a wealthy boyfriend who wanted to buy her an expensive birthday present. They had shopped together and selected a costly bracelet, but as this would have been difficult for Alice to explain to her husband, she and her boyfriend conspired with the jeweller to go along with the deception and quote George a much lower price.

What Are They?   36

House numbers.

The Keys   37

Andrew hadn't told Raymond that he was travelling to Bristol for a few days. Therefore Raymond had posted the keys to Andrew's Cambridge house, not realizing that they would be put through the mail slot in the door and that Andrew would then be unable to retrieve them in order to open the door.

Bank Robbery   38

The manager's assistant, in collusion with the cleaner, had taken a photograph of the safe, which had been blown up to life-size. This had been placed in front of the safe so that the guard could see only what he thought was the intact safe door. The cleaner removed the photograph when she arrived at the bank on Monday morning and disposed of it before anyone else arrived.

The Chairs   39

The upholsterer had discovered that gold coins had been hidden in each of the first three chairs and he was obviously eager to get his hands on the remaining three chairs and their contents.

Luxury Cruise   40

The Countess's necklace was in fact genuine and had been given to her by her rich lover. The Count had been told that the necklace was a well-made paste piece which the Countess had bought herself. Gerrard knew that the piece was genuine but, seeing the expression on the face of the Countess, he guessed the situation and gallantly lied and paid the Count.

Day Out   41

The social club members were travelling to Northville by train, and Mr. and Mrs. Jones decided to go to the dining car at the rear of the train for a quick snack.

In the Park   42

Sally was a Rottweiler bitch and the other dog was her mate.

Daily Routine   43

Joe is blind and has an arrangement with a shop assistant in the store to guide him across the busy street.

The Robbers   44

The "knowing" robber is in the habit of listening to his Walkman and, during jobs, tunes to the local police-calls station. Through the earphones, he had heard a police car being dispatched to the scene to investigate.

Suicide   45

Henry and Ann were obviously murdered, as the purported suicide note was grammatically incorrect. It should have read ". . . Ann and me." A philologist would not have made the mistake.

Police Emergency   46

The second police car had stalled in a tunnel so was unable to receive radio messages. They had therefore not heard the call for backup from the police station.

The Lovers   47

The rain had started early the previous evening. When Inspector Jones arrived at Pamela's house, he noticed that the ground underneath Paul Johnson's car was dry, so it had obviously not been moved since the day before. Paul had in fact overheard the telephone conversation with Peter and he and Pamela had had a violent argument. Paul had flown into a jealous rage and clubbed Pamela to death with a candlestick. He then waited until morning to telephone the police with the fake story.

The Punctures 48

The Mercedes was loaded on the train.

The Banker 49

When Inspector Brown pushed the play button the message had begun immediately. The tape had therefore been rewound, which could certainly not have been done by the dead man.

The Presidents 50

If the fifth U.S. president was not among those who died on that date, the newspaper item would almost certainly have made the more impressive statement that "Three of the first *four* presidents of the United States died on July 4th." Therefore, Tom was certain that the fifth president, James Monroe, died on that date.

Attica 51

Jaime had instantly realized, when Moses turned purple, that he was choking. He had first struck him on the back to try to dislodge the offending piece of food. When that had failed he had performed an emergency tracheotomy (opening the trachea, or windpipe, to provide a means of breathing when the natural air passage is obstructed above this level), thereby saving Moses' life.

Eyewitness 52

Claire Vermont viewed the murder from outside the house. She had just arrived home after an evening out when she spotted her butler committing the murder in her living room.

The Galaxy 53

The emerald the man was found clutching was a superb replica. He had swallowed the real gem and then emptied the flask of whiskey. He had been faking being inebriated before he smashed the crystal dome, but after he had drunk the contents of his hip flask, and by the time he was examined in the prison hospital, his blood alcohol level had risen very high.

The Menu 54

The couple are regular customers on the way to a show who have ordered an after-theater dinner.

A Job in a Million 55

Robert Bradley is chief steward in the first-class section, working for a world-famous airline.

The Thoroughbred 56

The other end of the rope isn't attached to anything.

The Crime 57

Suicide!

Homicide 58

Peter Collins was in fact a policeman. The trial had been a setup to enable him to gain the confidence of the Mafia contract killer and obtain evidence for a forthcoming Senate investigation.

The Blue Movie 59

Stephen was serious, he was head of the British Board of Film Censors.

Pools of Water 60

An organized street gang of youngsters had discovered an ingenious method to steal thousands of cigarettes, by freezing water into ice coins of a size which triggered the dispensing mechanism of the machines.

The Phone Rings 61

The meeting was a gathering of Mafia bosses. After welcoming the members, the boss of bosses told the meeting that one of them had broken the vow of *Omertà* (absolute silence) and had betrayed them. He then pretended that a high-level contact at the police would shortly telephone and identify the traitor.

Drink Drive 62

The man was acting as a decoy to draw the policemen away from the club, whose members, some of whom were more than slightly inebriated, drove off in a hurry as soon as the coast was clear.

Peril in the Air I 63

A window shattered and the passenger was sucked out of the plane.

Peril in the Air II 64

The plane had landed at the airport but had not yet arrived at the terminal.

The Mask 65

The man is a deep-sea diver. A diver at great depth can be affected by a phenomenon commonly referred to as "rapture of the deep." This condition causes euphoria, and the person afflicted loses grasp on reality and becomes convinced that equipment, such as the face mask, is useless and should be discarded.

The Venture 66

The two men were trying an Atlantic balloon crossing from New York to London which was heavily sponsored by a multi-national corporation. A sudden gust was blowing them towards a sky-scraper. A collision might have shattered their cabin, so to get a quick lift they had to jettison some of their sand-bag ballasts.

The Assassin 67

Eric was terminally ill and suffering intolerable pain. He had considered suicide, but the insurance policy on his life contained a suicide-exclusion clause. As Eric was determined to secure his family's financial future, he had hired a professional killer. His wife guessed what he had done and, for obvious reasons, did not want the killer to be apprehended.

The James Dean Appreciation Society 68

The fans were watching the movie on a charter jet from New York to the venue of the society's national convention. The air-craft suddenly developed engine trouble in-flight, and seemed about to crash when, just at the moment of the movie's sad climax, the pilot regained control.

Victoria Station 69

Brian was a bus driver. Bill was running to catch the bus, which he did, and thereafter became a passenger.

IRA Justice 70

The man had artificial legs and was therefore unhurt. He had only pretended to be in pain to allay suspicion—and likely additional shots to more vulnerable parts of his anatomy.

The Hundred-Dollar Note 71

Steve devised a method whereby he used fourteen $100 bills to make fifteen bills. He cut each of the notes into two parts as shown below (along the dotted lines). He then stuck the upper section (using clear adhesive tape) to the appropriate section of the next note with the result that fourteen bills became fifteen.

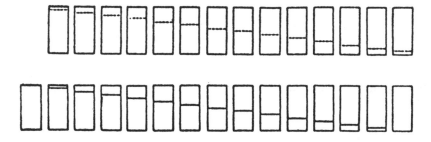

Each note was, of course, shortened by one-fifteenth of its length, which was not normally noticeable. (This trick was actually tried in pre-war Austria.)

The Operation 72

The man's son had been on a dialysis machine for years and his condition was deteriorating. Now his only partially working kidney was found to have a malignant growth and had to be removed. Although the doctors were still hoping to find a suitable donor for a transplant, the father decided not to risk further delay.

Double Homicide 73

The murderer was a forensic pathologist who lifted the fingerprints of a dead man on whom he had performed an autopsy and transferred them to the murder weapon. The corpse was then cremated, as per the family's wishes.

The Judgment 74

When the judge had asked what long-eared owl tasted like, the man had replied, "The taste of the owl was a cross between a golden condor and a bald eagle." (Both protected species.)

Discerning Shopper 75

She is a store employee. Part of her job is to remove items which will have gone beyond their "sell-by" date when the store opens the following morning.

The Lopsided Coins   76

There are probably several ways in which an equal chance could be achieved.

Since the coins are biased, the outcome of tossing one coin is obviously inequitable, but flipping both coins can result in:

Coin 1	Coin 2	
Heads	Heads	(HH)
Tails	Tails	(TT)
Heads	Tails	(HT)
Tails	Heads	(TH)

As HH is as equally likely to come up as TT, this could form the basis of a wager, whereby a flip producing HT and TH should be ignored.

Another solution would be to glue the two coins together in such a way that the biased faces are either touching or are at the outside of the fused coins, in which case the bias is eliminated by counterbalance.

The Slimming Pill   77

As is the standard procedure in testing medication, half the group were given placebos (dummy pills used as controls). All participants in the test were encouraged to indulge, to demonstrate the effectiveness of the pill without dieting. The recipients of the placebo therefore gained weight.

Pilot Error   78

Tim had served in the Royal Air Force for eighteen years and, after leaving, had decided to apply for a position as a commercial airline pilot. He had been training in a 747 flight simulator, and went on to become a full fledged British Airways pilot.

The Kangaroo Court   79

Hans was an undercover agent for the special anti-terrorist unit and had succeeded in infiltrating the cell. When the official was kidnapped and sentenced, Helldorf volunteered to perform the execution in order to save the man's life. He shot him with blanks; the blood was a "special effects" exercise with the props supplied by Hans. The newspapers were misled by the police to avoid blowing Helldorf's cover.

The Suspect   80

Brian devised what he considered a foolproof plan to cover his tracks. He had taped his conversation with Clifford on a previous afternoon visit with a tape recorder hidden in his briefcase. After killing Clifford he played the recording as he left the study for the benefit of the housekeeper. On rereading her testimony, the housekeeper suddenly realized that she had heard the grandfather clock chime six when the time was actually 11:00 p.m.

The System   81

Frank and Johnny were trying to launder drug money. One of the two would very likely show a substantial win at the end of the session, which would legitimate the cash he got for the chips. The compensating loss by his partner would go unnoticed. It is true that over a period of time the partnership would lose a small amount, about 1.35 percent, on the combined turnover, but in the long run the scheme would probably turn out cheaper, and certainly safer, than laundering through conventional channels.

Secrets of the Lake   82

The children had not drowned. Madelaine had taken them to a friend across the lake, in whom she had confided. Madelaine had hoped that her desperate charade would make René realize what might have happened and terminate the affair.

Madelaine could have been indicted for making a false report and wasting the time of the police, but in view of the circumstances she was not charged.

The Vandal   83

The restaurant owner had a slot machine installed on his premises by a criminal gang. A rival mob had forced him to install one of their machines, with guaranteed protection. When the original gang heard of the second machine they sent one of their heavies along to smash it up. After he left, the restaurant owner called the mob and told them what had happened, whereupon they eliminated the heavy.

Walking to the Park   84

Eric suffered from a compulsive obsession about cracks in the sidewalk; he would not step on them. To achieve this, he had to take exaggerated steps, which looked so odd. When he reached the park and could walk on the grass, his stride reverted to normal.

Nelson's Column   85

Rudolf's friend had decided to bungee jump from the top of Nelson's Column and had asked for the height so that he could arrange the correct length of elastic cord. Rudolf's miscalculation meant that his friend's rope was too long, thereby causing his death.

Witnesses for the Defense   86

Bruce and Harry were both monozygotic (identical) twins, and their defense lawyer had called their respective brothers. All four brothers had denied committing the robbery, and as the prosecution could not ascertain which pair of twins had actually committed the crime, the jury was forced to return a verdict of not guilty.

Foreign Exchange   87

The director of the central bank, new in his position, had instructed the designer to mark the artist's drawing with the word

"Specimen." As all the letters were in the Cyrillic alphabet, the printers failed to recognize this marking as a flaw.

Alerted to the "problem," the printer pointed out to the bank that the notes would become collectors' items and would probably sell at more than their face value.

The Hijack   88

The hijackers did not take the time to body-search their two victims, so they failed to notice that one had a cellular phone in the front pocket of his jacket. Despite the handcuffs, he managed, with the help of his co-worker, to get hold of the phone and dial 911. Speaking softly, he gave the police the truck's registration number and color, and by looking out of a small window he was able to describe the route taken by the culprits.

The Orchard   89

Bob Wilson lived on the 14th floor of a highrise. The orchard consisted of miniature fruit trees planted in pots on his balcony. When he went out to pick fruit, he tripped and fell over the balcony railing to his death below.

The Vacancy   90

Frank was having an affair with a young, married woman. She was the daughter of a diplomat born in Pakistan. As she spoke Urdu and French, the advertisement fit her like a glove. As her husband's salary was modest, he was more than happy to agree that his wife should accept this promising position, which enabled her to travel with her lover.

INDEX

Page key: puzzle name (**number**), puzzle, *clues*, **solution**.

About the Author

Erwin Brecher was born in Budapest and studied mathematics, physics, engineering, and psychology in Vienna, Brno (Czechoslovakia), and London.

He joined the Czech army in 1938 and, after the Nazi occupation of Sudetenland, he escaped to England. Engaged in aircraft design during the war, he later entered the banking profession, from which he retired in 1984. Currently, Erwin Brecher devotes his time to playing bridge and chess, and to writing books on scientific subjects or of puzzles, such as the recent *Journey Through Puzzleland*. His upcoming *Surprising Science Puzzles* encompasses several of his interests.

A member of Mensa, Erwin Brecher and his wife, Ellen, make their home in London, England.